A CENTURY OF
DOLLS

TREASURES FROM THE GOLDEN AGE OF DOLL MAKING

PHOTOGRAPHS BY TOM KELLEY · TEXT BY PAMELA SHERER

COURAGE
BOOKS
AN IMPRINT OF RUNNING PRESS
PHILADELPHIA · LONDON

Canadian representatives: General Publishing Co., Ltd.,
30 Lesmill Road, Don Mills, Ontario M3B 2T6

9 8 7 6 5 4 3 2 1
Digit on the right indicates the number of this printing.

Library of Congress Cataloging-in-Publication Number 94–73867

ISBN 1–56138–497–6

Cover and interior design by Frances J. Soo Ping Chow
Edited by Tara Ann McFadden
Pictures researched by Elizabeth Broadrup and Susan Oyama
Typography by Justin T. Scott

Published by Courage Books, an imprint of
Running Press Book Publishers
125 South Twenty-second Street
Philadelphia, Pennsylvania 19103–4399

ACKNOWLEDGMENTS

Tom Kelley gratefully acknowledges: Barbara Peters, Jo McKirihan, Michael Leonard, Corinne & Sara Burrell, Lucy & Clifford Cooney, Betty Gorgen, Barbara Ota, Marilyn Childs, Dottie Baker, Jackie Kaner, Joanne Egan, Joyce Olsen, Yvonne Lafond, Bobby & Cindy Hoskinson, Karen Vincent, Bea Ives, Helen Ragland, Eleanor & Renee Randazzo, Bulah Hawkins Doll Museum-John Hawkins, Nel Lucier, Dee Van Kampen, Christine Loreman, Beverly Butterfield, Millsteins General Store, Rod Norris, Norma Von Essen, Marie Coleman, Carol Platz, Barbara McWain, Helen Sieverling, Kay Jensen, Pat Gosh, Lilian Cameron, Marylou Edminston, Ruth Simons, Doris Dodge, Doris Libby, Julie Wright, Billie Nelson Tyrrell, Celina Carrol, Bea DeArmand, and special thanks to Harry van Bommel for making this project and the previous book project viable.

Pamela Sherer would like to thank Wiley, Sandy, and Kenzie Sherer for being good sports and thoroughly marvelous children; Ivonne Marin, for her patience and steady good humor; Allison Kurke; and Tony Sherer, for keeping his heart open to change.

INTRODUCTION

Tom Kelley's gorgeous photographs of antique dolls achieve something most photographs do not attempt: they present reality and fantasy simultaneously. He captures these fragile mementos, some nearly 125 years old, so that their remarkable physical presences and extraordinary craftsmanship shine through the pages. Yet, it is in his affinity for the dolls as they once were, as springboards for the imaginations of generations of little girls long ago grown up, that his work excels.

In these pages, an elegant use of color and cleverly designed settings invite the imagination of the reader; it is almost as though one could enter the scenes to sit down and play. Kelley's images create a sense of suspended time, in which the pressing requirements of modern life melt away and imagination and personal fancy take over.

Kelley explores the evocative potential of dolls from the heyday of European doll making in the late nineteenth century to the current era, including new creations from contemporary doll artists, and painstaking reproductions of extremely scarce antiques. With few exceptions, old and new alike have faces made of bisque, a term derived from "biscuit porcelain," which means unglazed porcelain.

By 1850, commercial production of carved wood dolls in Europe was giving way to "china" dolls with shiny glazed porcelain faces, painted eyes, and molded black hair.

These were not "dollies" as we now think of them, resembling young children or babies, but rather formal and somber-looking miniature women. Manufacturers would remodel hairdos every few years to reflect current fashion (and that is how collectors today can tell their approximate age), but generally, dolls looked much the same from about 1830 to 1860.

In the 1870s, styles changed. Interest in all sorts of porcelain, from tableware to decorative items helped to bring about a change in dolls. Simply put, they became lovelier, and so Tom Kelley has chosen dolls from this period to represent the oldest examples in this volume. Bisque, rather than glazed, porcelain was used for the most expensive dolls, which at first had fancy molded coiffures, decorated with ribbons, nets, and chignons. Today, this sort of design is referred to by collectors as "Parian" (see Plate #4) and features an elegant, mature-looking face.

This was also the era of the French fashion doll, similar to the "Parian," but with less emphasis on the modeling of porcelain details, and far more attention to elaborate silk gowns. The great French couturier Charles Frederick Worth would dispatch one of his chief designers to America in search of new clients, for whom the very latest fashions would be displayed in miniature on dolls.

By the mid 1880s, these refined mademoiselles had largely been replaced by the cherubic, enchanting faces of French *bébés,* whose undeniable appeal has not yet waned. Now highly prized by collectors and worth tens of thousands of dollars, their popularity is still rooted in their fragile beauty and expressiveness, which Tom Kelley's photographs evoke so well.

Gradually, the classic *bébé* evolved into a multitude of more realistic designs, depicting young children, babies, and newborns, some laughing or even crying. Highly productive German manufacturers took over the international market, exporting their adorable, mischievous-looking wares all over the globe.

Newcomers to the world of antique dolls can explore more of the history behind these charming faces by delving into some of the references listed on page 128, especially the two volumes of *The Collector's Encyclopedia of Dolls,* without which many an expert would feel lost. But novices and seasoned collectors alike will want to come back again and again to the glorious images on the following pages, to look, learn, escape, and imagine. Fair warning! You may lose all track of time as you turn these pages!

—Pamela Sherer

#1

Caught in a nostalgic moment, this mademoiselle's inward gaze draws us in as well. There is something quiet and contemplative found in the faces of French *bébés*. The full, softly modeled cheeks have the appeal of a chubby toddler, yet the large, dark eyes seem older. Probably made in the mid 1880s by the Parisian firm of François Gaultier, she is a good example of French manufacture during the last quarter of the nineteenth century, which is often referred to as the golden age of doll making.

Some characteristics to look for are a very finely textured matte bisque, or unglazed porcelain; wide set, lustrous glass eyes; and a jointed neck and body. After more than a hundred years, a doll's clothing has usually been replaced, but in this case, her dress may be original, although the high-button kid boots are not.

Of all the hundreds of different styles of dolls made in France in the late nineteenth century, perhaps this face is the perfect archetype. The classic hallmarks are there: the large, luminous eyes, the delicate complexion, the broad chubby cheeks and dimpled chin, even the pierced ears. Although the porcelain is terribly fragile, this doll has been so well cared for that not a crack has appeared.

Anyone with a good eye would suspect that here is a treasure, and even collectors new to the field might recognize the classic loveliness of this Jumeau doll dating from the 1890s. The company begun by Pierre François Jumeau about 1842 in Montreuil-sous-Bois, outside Paris, became a giant in its field. Dolls carrying the name held a special cachet, then as now, much like Tiffany and Company has come to represent the highest standards of quality in jewelry.

#2

#3

I n the early years of the Maison Jumeau (literally, House of Jumeau), heads for their dolls were purchased from other firms, including François Gaultier (see Plate #1). By the early 1870s, however, Pierre Jumeau had set up his own porcelain operation. In 1873, he was joined by his son Emile, and it was then that the firm started its world-renowned rise.

Some of the earlier heads made by Jumeau during this period are not fully marked; some bear only size numbers. Such designs are usually referred to now as "portrait" Jumeaux, although it is not thought that they were meant to represent a specific person. The face, while softly modeled, does not have the look of a young child that would characterize the later *bébés*, as seen in Plate #2. This equestrienne is a regal 34 inches tall.

Parian is the classification now used by collectors for this type of doll from the 1860s and 1870s. The term refers to Greek marble, but is meant to emphasize the flawless, finely grained texture of the bisque. Many of this type were made in Germany, already a well-established producer of exceptional porcelain wares. Developing dolls as a sideline must have been a natural diversification, for a few dozen German firms, mostly from the Thür region, became enormously successful by the turn of the century.

While some were marked with numbers or letters, probably to identify one design from another, the specific makers of Parian dolls are not usually known. Notice that the doll's eyes are painted on, rather than made of glass and inset, and her face is decidedly womanly, rather than childlike. It is not uncommon for a Parian to have pierced ears, but the more elaborate the coiffure—some include ribbons, bows, and snoods—the more desirable the doll becomes to collectors today.

#4

Concurrent with the production of Parian dolls in Germany, fashion dolls were the dominant trend in France. These are characterized by a more blushed complexion, a wig rather than molded hair, and a body often made of white kid leather with gusset joints to provide some flexibility. This elegant example has a rarer type of body made by the Parisian company, Gesland. It features a wire armature within soft, stuffed stockinet limbs with bisque hands, and is considered to add substantially to its value today. The heads of fashion dolls are only occasionally marked with a maker's name or initials, so this sophisticated lady is unidentifiable.

In some cases, this sort of doll was less a plaything than a miniature mannequin, for she was sumptuously dressed to show off the latest Paris fashions. Even the undergarments would be trimmed with the lace, the tiny boots would actually button, and silk and satin were *de riguer*.

#6

In the late 1860s and early 1870s, Léon Casimir Bru had already had some success in producing fashion dolls. This serene example's necklace disguises a swivel joint in her neck. Within ten years, however, the style had shifted to the youthful proportions of the *bébé*, and it was the lavish craftsmanship of the firm's various styles that attracted international attention.

This *bébé* is marked only with a dot within a circle, but doll collectors will instantly recognize the inimitable face of a Bru. The subtle, blushed tinting of the bisque, the light brushstroked eyebrows and eyelashes, the slight parting of the lips, and softly dimpled fingers are all hallmarks of a *Bru Jeune*. She wears her original ice blue satin afternoon frock with matching hat. Underneath, her bisque shoulders are molded in a piece separate from the head, with a kid-lined joint at the base of the neck; the rest of the body is white kid leather.

#7

#8

After the previous *bébé,* this slightly later German doll makes a telling comparison. Her shoulders and head are molded in a single piece, the eyes are proportionately smaller and not as deep, and her hands, while bisque, show somewhat cursory modeling. Because of mass production and limited hand detailing by craftsmen, German doll manufacturers were able to produce much less expensive dolls that nevertheless bore some resemblance to their fantastically expensive French cousins.

This fifteen-inch tall lady was created by Alt, Beck & Gottschalck, a firm that is now thought to have specialized in making glazed porcelain doll heads and the Parian-type doll with molded hair.[1] By the 1880s, it was normal for both French and German doll makers to patent their designs and innovations, and to mark their creations with identifying mold numbers and/or maker's name or initials. The mold and size numbers 915 #5 can be found incised on the back of this doll's head.

Representing different generations in nineteenth-century doll design, the fashion lady on the left was created by François Gaultier, a thriving firm that went on to make its own line of *bébés*. (For an example, look back at Plate #1; hardly a trace of a family resemblance remains.) Her dress and kid leather hands are modern restorations.

Her walking companion is incised "E11J" on the back of the neck. This refers to Emile Jumeau, who joined his father's company in 1873 and proceeded to build Maison Jumeau into one of the most prominent doll makers in the world. Emile's wife, Ernestine, took charge of costume design in the mid 1870s,[2] designing beribboned, lace-trimmed confections that were astonishingly detailed. Jumeau dolls were famous for their extravagant ensembles of cashmere, satin, velvet, silk taffeta, and brocade. Maison Jumeau took such pride in its creations even their tiny doll shoes bore a company mark.

#9

#10

Although there was only a short history of doll manufacture in France in the first half of the nineteenth century, in the second half a thriving business developed remarkably quickly. Then as now, nothing succeeds like success—and so doll companies copied each other's designs, just as they do today.

The two petite mademoiselles in this parlor scene seem to bear quite a family resemblance, but even such charming appearances can deceive. These dolls were made by fiercely competitive companies. The larger one is stamped *"Tête Jumeau,"* (head by Jumeau), while the smaller one is incised "A-3," an identifying mark of the Jules Steiner firm of Paris. They were probably made within a few years of each other, between 1890 and 1900.

#11

However fetching the bisque face, doll makers also needed to be concerned with the type of body for the doll. Stuffed cloth would be the least expensive, but was not particularly strong, and did not provide much flexibility for posing. French fashion dolls often had white or pink kid bodies with gusset joints. Some from about 1870 had carved wood bodies, which allowed for both strength and a full complement of joints, but were costly to produce.

In the late 1870s, composition ball-jointed bodies became the norm. The pale beauty illustrated here, from the French company Jules Steiner, jauntily holds her original parasol, showing her typical composition arms. "Composition" is a catch-all word for many types of composite materials, but in doll terms, composition usually indicates a moldable amalgam quite like papier-mâché. The individual parts of the limb would be made separately, then strung together with cord.

This poised French bisque lady seems to take such delight in her collection of Victorian Valentines, which epitomize the decorative complexity popular in that era. Her gaze is so compelling that it draws our eyes away from the fine touches of craftsmanship that make up the rest of her face. A closer look reveals that the blush of her cheeks, the outline of her lips, her eyelashes, and eyebrows, are all painted—by hand—with deft, light strokes. Look again, and you will notice that her eyebrows are not quite identical, just as no living human face is precisely symmetrical.

For those who have not already guessed her identity, *"Tête Jumeau"* is stamped in red at the back of her neck. Her wig and pink satin ensemble with ruched trim is new, though skillfully made in a turn-of-the-century style. When a wonderful doll such as this outlives her original clothing, it seems only right to replace it in high style.

#12

#13

The training of a refined young lady always included instruction in the arts, especially music, for what more suitable finale to a lovely soirée could there be than a brief musical interlude played by a talented mademoiselle? In fact, the phonograph was already well-developed by the end of the nineteenth century. The ever ingenious Maison Jumeau even concealed small phonographs in the torsos of some of their dolls!

The attentive *poupée* (French for doll) pictured here has the characteristic broad face of a Jules Steiner doll. She is incised "C 6." The "C" identifies a series of molds that Steiner used; the "6" is a size number. If you have an odd sense of déjà-vu when you see her face, good for you! Just turn back one page to see another C-series Steiner. Our musical friend is also marked "Paris *Bébé*."

These two French *bébés* by the Parisian firm Schmitt & Fils (fils is French for son) look as if they are related. Each seems to have its own distinct appearance and personality, which is ironic considering that these charming playmates were produced in large numbers for many years.

But a carefully crafted doll is different than a well-made tin toy from the same period. Both became more attainable because of the burgeoning industrial revolution and an ever-growing middle class, but the toy will always seem one step closer to mass production, because, quite simply, it doesn't have a lifelike face. And an antique doll, with its smooth bisque skin and luminous eyes, has a direct appeal that skips right past logic to lodge in the heart. It is this essential trick of the human mind, to find irresistible fascination in a face, that underlies our captivation with dolls down through the millennia.

The subtle, inward gaze of this blue-eyed beauty is typical of *bébés* made by Bru. Her body, however, is unusual. Notice that her head is cocked slightly to one side. Bru *bébés* always had jointed necks, but underneath her light-catching gown, she has a bisque shoulderplate, complete with molded bosom. Her torso is kid, with lower arms of celluloid, and lower legs of wood. Clearly, she was made during a time of experimentation and innovation in doll design.

The various doll companies were eager to display these innovations at the international trade exhibitions, in the hope of winning awards they could then trumpet in their advertisements. Bru, owned by H. Chevrot, won no fewer than ten gold medals between 1885 and 1889.[3] The firm also patented numerous designs, including *Bébé Têteur* (Nursing Baby) and *Le Dormeur* (The Sleeper), as well as supposedly unbreakable models. "Breveté" or its abbreviation "Bte" (French for patented) are marks often found on French dolls.

The late 1800s was a time of extraordinary invention, from the telephone to the electric light bulb, although many proved less enduring. New ways of mechanically reproducing music were much sought after, especially devices where one could easily change the tune. (Then-current Swiss methods of making music boxes were very time consuming, and only a small number of tunes were permanently installed on each roll.) That may be why this bevy of French *bébés* is clustered around the very latest in mechanical music, a German-made Polyphon from about 1905 that plays interchangeable metal discs.

Have you already tried to identify these faces? From left to right, they are Jumeau, Jumeau, Bru, Jumeau, and Bru. The last one has her dimpled bisque hand on the crank of the music box, showing its careful modeling and silky smooth bisque. You may want to turn back a page to compare this design to the hands of the dreamy Bru in Plate #15.

#16

Doll historians have sifted through municipal archives and enormous numbers of nineteenth-century periodicals to ferret out clues as to how these pale beauties were made and marketed. When it comes to a *Tête Jumeau,* such as the thoughtful one posed here, a researcher's mind veers away from fantasy toward fact. A face suggestive of contemplation and tenderness becomes an illustration of the handiwork of artisans in the service of market forces demanding quality and a more appealing product. This sort of analytical approach has provided collectors and appraisers with quite useful criteria by which to judge dolls. In the mid 1870s, when Emile Jumeau joined his father's firm and expanded the company's line with *bébés* rather than *poupées,* or fashionable ladies, the custom was to press the rather doughlike bisque into the mold of a doll's head. Toward the end of the century, with German methods giving the French a run for their money, the faster technique of pouring a more liquid slip into the mold became the norm.

#18

Here, another beguiling Jumeau proves the point long trumpeted in ladies' magazines that accessories are everything. Her watered silk dress, sprigged with roses, a jabot of cream lace at her neck, is original, as are her blue bead earrings and her enameled gilt brooch proudly proclaiming *"Bébé."* It was not uncommon for such a fancy young lady to have a matching ivory-handled parasol for each separate outfit in her trousseau, as well as a selection of white, brown, and black high-button boots and coordinated kid gloves to choose from. To a certain extent, dolls can be approximately dated by their original costumes. For this purpose, *The Collector's Encyclopedia of Doll Clothes,* with its multitude of reproduced early advertisements, is invaluable, although a doll's marks and physical appearance are always defining factors.

When collectors or professional dealers appraise an antique doll like this, what do they look for? First, what company made it and how is it marked? What is its condition? To ascertain that, the bisque head must be searched for cracks, as even the faintest hairline fracture will reduce its value by at least two-thirds. And porcelain restorers can do an excellent job repairing a chipped neck socket. Hold the head up to a strong light, looking for anomalies in the surface finish. Better yet, stick a penlight *inside* the head, if the wig is loose; cracks should show up immediately. Are all the parts original to the doll? (Doll "hospitals," as doll repair shops are commonly called, have been faithfully replacing an arm here, a leg there, for generations. Check for appropriate proportion and different colored parts on the body. As in this case, wigs are often replaced.) Only after these basic questions have been answered can rarity and value be considered.

#19

#20

Not much is known about Rabery & Delphieu, the Parisian doll maker to which credit goes for this pensive harpist, who is incised "RD 3" on the back of her neck. At 25 inches in height, she is a fairly large *bébé*. It was the custom for European doll firms to offer each model in a range of sizes, usually from about 10 inches to about three feet tall. A little girl could also choose a doll with luxurious clothes, merely fancy clothes, or a simple lace-trimmed slip called a chemise, and then practice her stitchery by making clothes herself. There was thus a doll to be had for almost every budget. The German *poupées* tended to be less expensive, while the lavishly bedecked French ones could be outrageously costly, especially when they came equipped with several different silk or satin dresses. Undoubtedly, this particular young lady would have been on the expensive side.

Every passionate collector dreams of poking about in an attic and lifting the lid of an old trunk to discover treasures like these, but it doesn't often happen that way with dolls. Because of their original expense, early bisque dolls were considered treasures right from the beginning. A doll would often be named by her lucky young owner and played with gingerly, even infrequently, to protect the fragile bisque. She was likely to be passed down to the next generation as a highly prized memento. Even dolls who were played with so much that they fell apart (the cord strung through all the body parts was apt to break), would be carefully gathered and kept in a safe place until the time came for the disorganized jumble to be ceremoniously carried off to a doll hospital for restoration.

#21

#22

What complements a peaches-and-cream complexion better than antique lace? This delightful early *bébé* looks fresh and lovely in her afternoon ensemble as she searches her hatboxes for just the right accessory. What a lucky find, to discover a doll so well-kept, after the trials and tribulations of a century or so.

But there's a catch! This is not her original outfit at all, but a new costume artfully made out of period fabrics, with such detail and skillful fitting that it suits her to a "T." Or should one say "J," for this is a Jumeau, as you may already have recognized. Her body is certainly original (note the typically flexed position of her composition hands), and her curly blond wig looks quite close to the sort of lamb's wool coiffure she might have had once. She stands 18 inches tall.

This winsome Jumeau looks like she has never stepped out of her first home, but in fact she is rather well-traveled. Some time before the turn of the century, she was shipped over to the United States from France, perhaps to be sold at one of the great department stores of the day, such as R. H. Macy's or F. A. O. Schwarz. Where she spent the next seven or eight decades is lost information, but one thing is certain: she was very well cared for. All her clothes are original, as you may have guessed from the elegant embroidery on her silk dress.

Her current owner, a California collector and doll dealer named Barbara Ota, found her in the catalog of a well-known doll auctioneer. Ms. Ota's long experience in the doll field enabled her to notice that the pre-sale auction estimate for this Jumeau had been accidentally switched with the doll next to it in the catalog—instead of $7,000, it was printed as $4,000! Barbara went to the sale to bid in person, hoping against hope that the auction house wouldn't notice their mistake—and neither would a couple of hundred other savvy collectors. Not all collecting stories have such a happy ending, but this time, as she puts it, Barbara was *"Tremendously* lucky!"

#23

\#24

Just a last glance in the mirror, and another pretty Jumeau is ready for her afternoon outing. Comparing her with the preceding Jumeau *bébé,* you will notice a few key variations. Notice that her flounced dress with its peach satin bows is a new one, her wrists are jointed, and her mouth is open, with a delicate row of straight little teeth. In details like these, you can detect the enormous competitive pressure on the French doll makers from their increasingly successful German counterparts, who were adding more realistic details to their dolls at a steady pace.

Open-mouthed dolls, who seem so alive as if they were about to engage you in conversation, were once thought of as an improvement, so open mouths became a standard feature. Millions upon millions were produced. Ironically, a century later, their open mouths mark them as more common to devoted collectors, and thus less valuable in today's market.

A similar open-mouthed Jumeau (see Plate #24) sits down for a tête-à-tête with a German contemporary named Daisey. Now fast friends, the rivalry between their makers is long forgotten.

Daisey is the product of J. D. Kestner, one of the most important of the German doll companies. Kestner was based in the Thür region of Germany, where there was a concentration of porcelain manufacturers. She is charming proof that makers like Kestner created dolls of excellent quality. Hers is a classic "dolly" face, with an open mouth and sleeping eyes that opened and closed by means of a counterweight inside the head. Indeed, it is in the eyes that there is most difference between these two bisque dolls. Jumeau and many other French doll makers continued to use thick glass eyes because they caught the light so well, imparting a lifelike animation to each face. Because of the depth of the glass, they are now called "paperweight" eyes.

#26

Meet Evangeline, who has been passed down in the same family ever since she was originally purchased. At 30 inches tall, she is the size of a real toddler, but certainly no real toddler could keep her dress so clean while making Christmas cookies! Her sturdy, ball-jointed composition body makes it easy to pose her in different positions, and her counterweighted sleeping eyes stay wide open when she stands up.

She was christened Evangeline by her family, not by Simon & Halbig, the German doll company that made her probably between 1900 and 1910. Simon & Halbig not only sold a wide variety of dolls under their own name, but supplied bisque heads to at least a dozen other firms. Their output was of such good quality that even Jumeau used them during this period, when a number of the leading French doll companies merged to form the Société Française de Fabrication de Bébés et Jouets, or S. F. B. J.

Simon & Halbig also gets the credit for this Belton-type doll. In the highly specialized nomenclature that has grown up in the doll world, "Belton" refers to a technique of molding a bisque head whole. Most bisque heads have a cut-away back to make it easier to set in the eyes; the space is then filled in with a cork, plaster, or cardboard pate, to which the wig is glued.) The Beltons have just the top back part of the head slightly flattened and pierced with two holes.

Although the majority of closed mouth Simon & Halbig Belton-types have composition childlike bodies, the one illustrated here has a lady-style kid body with bisque hands. This is the level of hidden detail that doll devotees must master!

#28

The German firm of J. D. Kestner created this pensive bride. Incised on the back of her head with the mold number 11, she is distinguished by her closed mouth and by the way her head is turned to the side in a fixed position above her bisque shoulderplate, as is the similar redhead. The latter, however, has an open mouth individually inset with four pearly teeth, a feature that young girls in 1895 or so would have enjoyed. Both have gusseted kid bodies with nicely modeled bisque lower arms and hands. (Earlier fashion dolls often had kid arms, too, but leather hands, even with individually stitched fingers, looked rather clumsy.) Because dolls like these could not turn their heads, this type of one-piece shoulderhead was soon superceded by more fully jointed composition designs.

#29

Lost in her thoughts, this lovely bisque face is the epitome of the classic German "dolly." It jars the modern sensibility to think of her as an assemblage of individual parts, yet an 1888 account of the doll manufacturing cottage industry in Waltershausen, Germany makes interesting reading.

"Old, young, big, small, men, women—all are hard at work with dolls. Factories . . . are used to assemble the dolls. Individual parts flow into these factories from all over the country. Many people who live in villages carve arms or legs, shape heads or bodies or turn joints on lathes. This goes on from morning till night in house after house. At the end of the school day, children help out. There are bodies to stuff and sew up, often for only a few cents per dozen. When everyone helps, they assemble and work together.

"Where painters live, racks of freshly painted doll heads are seen in windows of houses and along garden fences. One painter is a master painter and specializes in lips and dimples. Another has learned to paint eyes and arching brows. A row of other painters dip individual limbs into flesh-color glue. On Saturday morning, everything is loaded into wheelbarrows and taken to the city to sell."[4]

#30

#31

In the late nineteenth century, nearly all little girls learned to sew, just like this 21-inch tall German doll by Kestner. Patterns for new doll outfits were a popular feature of several periodicals of the time, including *Harper's Bazaar* and *McCall's*. Patterns could also be purchased from Butterick for all manners of clothing, from French-styled dresses down to simple chemises. Stitching together fetching ensembles from leftover bits of cloth from the sewing basket or rag bag was considered excellent practice. A girl might make a sailor suit, a pinafore, or a hooded riding cloak, or perhaps a new set of under-garments with flounced drawers and a camisole.

Collectors these days take great pride in dolls still wearing their original dresses and become nearly ecstatic if a doll is found in its original box. The aspiring seamstress pictured here has been redressed in modern times, but the brooch of gold-washed stamped tin she wears, saying Darling, dates from the same period as the doll.

With a faraway look in her big blue paperweight eyes, this French *bébé* by Jullien is dressed in a pale ecru lace threaded with powder-pink satin ribbons that set off her complexion quite nicely. Doll experts learn to recognize a certain smoothness, or pale creamy-looking bisque, as more typical of earlier French dolls. Bisque with a slight sheen (described by collectors as "oily") is considered very desirable. Around the turn of the century, when the great French doll makers banded together as the Société Française de Fabrication de Bébés et Jouets, doll cheeks were often heavily blushed, even ruddy, and refined painted details such as eyelashes became more slap-dash. Jullien joined the S. F. B. J. about 1904.[5] This faithful correspondent was probably made during the preceding decade.

Jullien dolls are clearly marked with the full name, not just initials. At 19 inches in height, she is probably a Jullien size 6.

#32

#33

The original Johann Daniel Kestner of Waltershausen, Germany, started his business in 1805, long before these dolls were made. In the midst of the Napoleonic wars, he traded with the troops for various small necessities; by 1823, the company was making papier-mâché dolls, as well as buttons and notebooks. The German railroad reached Waltershausen in 1848 making the shipment of dolls faster and more cost efficient. This set up the conditions for a healthy export trade which was already booming by the time his grandson, Adolf Kestner, took charge of the thriving firm in 1863.[6]

A more elegant nursemaid than this 26-inch tall Kestner is hard to imagine. She is marked with the size number 16, and is characteristic of the style of doll popular from about 1885 to 1890. Her animated young charge is a later character baby, with the incised mark "JDK 257." He was probably made around 1915.

Another charming Kestner design, this doll exhibits what collectors call an "open/closed" mouth, meaning that the lips are carefully painted to seem slightly apart, further animating her face, with its brown sleep eyes. She is incised "#11," and measures 18 inches in height.

Her elegant russet brocade afternoon dress, with its trimmings of ruched ribbon and lace and a matching broad-brimmed bonnet, bespeaks a gentler time, when a proper young lady was expected to adhere to a long list of expectations—in attire and comportment—when venturing out into the public eye. Outfits like this one, inspired by old patterns and made of period lace and fabrics, cost more than many women would want to spend for themselves, much less for a doll. Price tags of $300 to $450 are no longer uncommon for intricate ensembles appropriately fitted and hand-stitched throughout. Only a decade ago, that kind of money bought you the doll as well!

#35

The West Coast woman who cares for this serene brown-eyed *Tête Jumeau* started collecting about twenty years ago, after finding an old doll in her grandmother's basement. The doll was literally in pieces, so she had it restrung and redressed. The results were gorgeous, and she found herself intrigued by the collection she saw at the restorer's. She started going to antique doll shows, and eventually joined a doll collectors' club. While she says she's learned a great deal in two decades of collecting, no matter what the rarity of a doll, it still needs to have a pretty face before she'll buy it. She has sold a few dolls along the way in order to trade up for better ones, and from this experience she mentions a gentle warning for newcomers to the field: variations on the "I found this in my grandmother's basement" story seem to be proliferating, and sometimes need to be taken with a grain of salt!

I ronically, one of the most recognizable Jumeau designs does not bear the famous maker's name. This is the *Jumeau Triste*, which translates from the French as "Sad Jumeau," but is usually referred to as the "long-face Jumeau" by collectors. The face was created in 1879 by the sculptor A. E. Carrier de Belleuse, who had been commissioned by the Maison Jumeau to render "the ultimate doll."[7] Marked only with a size number on the back of the head, these *Jumeaux Tristes* are fairly large; this one measures 28 inches tall.

Producing a wistful doll seems not to have been a wildly successful business decision for Jumeau, for although they were produced for some years, they survive in relatively small numbers. This scarcity, of course, enhances their desirability today. At public auction, such a doll might be estimated to bring close to $20,000, or even more if it is in pristine condition in its original dress.

#36

Fresh and ready for an afternoon's ride, this mademoiselle stands expectantly beside her miniature antique carriage as though she were awaiting an outing to the Tuileries, perhaps. She is marked a Paris *Bébé*, with the trademark of the Eiffel Tower stamped on her body. Danel & Cie first registered the Paris *Bébé* in 1889. If you notice a strong resemblance to Jumeau *bébés*, so did Maison Jumeau! Danel had previously been employed by Jumeau and was successfully sued for copying their designs, "borrowing" molds, and making off with Jumeau employees. Such was Jumeau's power in its field that Danel & Cie remains just a footnote, despite having made about 50,000 of these beautiful *bébés* per year.[8]

When your last name is Bru, you can afford to be photographed in your corset and pantaloons, selecting your accessories for the day. Bru used many different styles of body over the years, but collectors prize this type of characteristic carved and turned wood body because of its sturdiness, attention to details such as the toes, and its jointed ankles and wrists. Kid gloves, an original brooch, and a lacy parasol are natural accompaniments for a doll whose name is synonymous with luxury.

Which of her outfits should she choose? A *bébé* from the 1890s might have had a drop-waisted sateen dress with a gathered ribbon sash above a box-pleated, lace-edged skirt, perhaps with a silk-lined fine wool capelet outlined in fancy metallic braid to keep her shoulders warm. Rich colors including wine-red, chestnut brown, and deep green were often chosen for an appealing contrast with the pale, gently blushed bisque complexion of a good *bébé*. Today's doll designers, so addicted to the hot pink of the Barbie age, could do well to look back a hundred years for more subtle color inspirations.

#38

Already helping with the next generation, this 1890s petite *jeune fille* (little girl) is a sizable *Bru Jeune* 12 who stands 30 inches tall. Her young charge is a German character baby made by J. D. Kestner in the 1910s; the back of his neck is incised with the identifying mold number 211. Both dolls feature composition bodies, but the Bru's is fully ball-jointed. When character infant dolls became popular after 1910, an appropriate five-piece body type was developed, with a short, chubby torso and bent arms and legs. Sleeping eyes that opened and closed by means of a counterweight concealed in the head were by that time a standard feature.

Less expensive, machine-made lace was widely available in the 1890s, and more dolls began to be dressed in fine white cotton lawn with lace inserts and trim, in longer dress lengths than had been fashionable for girl dolls in the 1880s.

#39

#40

The size range of most antique dolls is generally the same as the majority of dolls today, in the neighborhood of one to two feet tall, such as this luminescent French *bébé* by Schmitt, who measures 22 inches from curly blond mohair wig to composition toe. Her pale blue paperweight eyes, open/closed mouth, and creamy bisque complexion date her to about 1885.

Very large dolls were more expensive originally and made in fewer numbers, two factors which increase their desirability in today's competitive doll market. On the right, the impressive Bru boy stands a full 38 inches tall. His fully jointed wood arms and hands are quite like those used as artists' models, rather than the ball-jointed composition limbs customary at this time. His quiet companion is also French, incised "F. G." for François Gaultier.

All three of these *bébés* have the characteristics one would expect from late nineteenth-century French doll makers, and determining their ages entails a certain amount of educated guesswork. It is helpful to remember that Schmitt & Fils went out of business in 1891, while Gaultier and Bru continued to combat fierce German competition throughout the decade, finally joining forces with Jumeau and other firms in 1899 to form the Société Française de Fabrication de Bébés et Jouets.

#41

This diminutive pair looks for all the world like twins, but again, maker's marks on the back of their necks tell a different story. Looking natty in his straw boater is a so-called American Schoolboy, with molded blond hair and a closed mouth. He hails from Germany, however, as denoted by his marks "C. O. D. 30 B 1½ Germany." The initials C. O. D. in the doll world do not mean cash-on-delivery (although a little 11-inch schoolboy like this is certainly valuable), but stand instead for Cuno & Otto Dressel, a successful firm of considerable longevity in Sonneburg.

Beside him is a petite French girl in a fresh red-checked suit made by her owner, who started collecting dolls as a girl herself when she talked her mother into buying her a doll from *Gone With the Wind* by Madame Alexander in 1937. This little beauty's long, pointed fingers are a clue to her identity: she's a Steiner, with an additional stamped mark from the famous Parisian retailer, *Au Nain Bleu*, which in its day was the F. A. O. Schwarz in Europe.

#42

#43

Expressly designed for the United States market,[9] "Lilly," as she is marked, was made in Köppelsdorf, Germany by Armand Marseille, an enormously productive doll company which molded bisque-head dolls by the millions around the turn of the century. Her head and shoulders are made in one piece, called a shoulderhead by collectors, which is attached to a kid body with bisque lower arms.

For the most part, Armand Marseille dolls were never intended to compete with the luxurious French *bébés*, but were the sort of modest, inexpensive dollies that middle class families all over the world could afford. Her eyebrows are painted each with a swift, single stroke, her head cannot turn, yet that did not matter to hundreds of thousands of girls who simply used their imaginations to fill in the special details of their dreams.

Simon & Halbig of Germany gets the credit for both of these charming bisque dolls. At the left is a character dolly from their 900 series, begun in the late 1880s. She is incised "929" and stands 19 inches tall.

Never mind if this young girl's dress (at right,) is showing a bit of wear here and there—she is lucky to have her original silk dress and bonnet. Her finely textured pale bisque is marked 1079—a mold also used by Simon & Halbig to supply heads for the illustrious Maison Jumeau.

Simon & Halbig was the major employer in the small town of Gräfenhain where they established their porcelain factory in 1869 and began to produce dolls about a decade later. Carl Halbig was a compassionate local leader. German doll historians Marianne and Jürgen Cieslik note that Halbig "had ice skates distributed to the children in wintertime . . . he ordered lamps installed and the streets illuminated at night; and he always paid for the food for the school children, in good and in bad times."[10]

#46

Southern California collector Barbara Peters has a special fondness for Tom Kelley's photographs of her dolls, for they are all that remains of her collection. All but one of the dolls she lovingly gathered over decades of collecting managed to survive the harrowing earthquake of 1994. They "danced" around in their glass-fronted cases, and a few hats and wigs went askew, yet only a Bye-lo baby was broken.

On the very next day, the unthinkable happened. Electrical damage caused by the earthquake started an unstoppable fire that destroyed what the earthquake had only disarranged. This adorable chubby toddler by Kammer & Reinhardt, Simon & Halbig (Simon & Halbig supplied the heads for several Kammer & Reinhardt's character dolls, hence the names of both companies appearing on many *K* ✡ *R* characters, including the mold numbers 115, 116, and 117) was one of dozens and dozens of antique dolls that were loved for decades but perished in a moment or two. In the best spirit of doll collectors, Mrs. Peters only wishes she had had more time to share them with others.

There is always more to learn about antique dolls and the world they came from. Posing this 26-inch German bisque-head dolly in a student setting is apt because of the historical expectations for children to be diligent learners and apply themselves seriously to any task at hand. In a small booklet originally published in 1834 in Massachusetts entitled *A Present for Good Children*, a young girl is seated under an arbor of climbing roses, looking up from her reading at her approaching brother. The brief story is titled "Robert and His Sister."

Little Robert, tired of trundling his hoop, has come to the arbour where his sister is reading, to talk with her. They are both obedient children, and love each other much. They sometimes play at innocent amusements, but never against the will of their friends, or when they should be at school. When they are not at play they are never idle, but are always engaged in working or reading.

This is doing what is right. Children should learn to be industrious, and store their minds with useful knowledge.[11]

#47

Although she is about 100 years old, this mademoiselle looks young and fresh. While most of the French *bébés* were meant to represent children as opposed to adults, the faces seem indeterminate in age. The style of its clothing often gave more clues as to the envisioned age of a doll. For boy dolls—and yes, they were made every year by the tens of thousands—long or short pants were the giveaway, and sailor suits or military uniforms were popular.

This young lady is wearing an appropriate, if not original, white cotton lawn day dress, with a lace jabot and double-tiered, lappet-edged sleeves. She stands 24 inches tall and is incised with the F. G. scroll mark attributed to François Gaultier of France. Her relatively long, tapered composition fingers make her instrument a natural choice. Pianos such as this miniature were a classic child's toy through the 1930s.

No matter what one's age, as a child or as a collector, a leit-motif of doll play is to project one's own nurturing fantasies onto a doll caring for another doll. The grown-up in this case is an Emile Jumeau that measures 17 inches in height. Her head is marked with a size number 6, and her blond mohair wig perfectly complements her pale, peachy complexion and wide-set blue paper-weight eyes.

In her arms, she holds an all-bisque baby just 4 inches in length, which, despite its diminutive size, has sleeping eyes that open and close, jointed shoulders and hips, and molded black shoes. In evaluating small dolls, collectors look especially for fully jointed examples, rather than the inexpensively produced glazed-china "frozen Charlottes" whose bodies were all molded in one piece, with the arms bent forward at the elbows. At the other end of the spectrum, prices of up to $1,000 are not unheard of for deftly made French all-bisques just a few inches tall.

#49

This Bru's face expresses a lively sense of anticipation; her blue eyes seem so focused and expectant that the imaginary bird song could almost be real. The impression that the doll is just about to gasp with delight is in part a result of the modeling of her mouth, which is set with the lips slightly parted, and just the line of her upper teeth showing. This lifelike "open/closed mouth" design feature is sought after by collectors.

Despite the importance of modeling and smooth, creamy bisque in a doll's face, it is the eyes which communicate the most, suggesting a mood, catching the light, or slowly closing as the treasured plaything is tucked away for a rest. Doll makers naturally vied to produce new, more expressive, and novel eye designs to give their dolls that special something extra that would appeal to the coming generation of little girls. This and the following three photographs illustrate different approaches to eye design.

Distinctively broad faces are a hallmark of French *bébés* by Jules Steiner, of which this C-series is a fetching example in her antique embroidered claret silk dress. Compare this young lady with the Steiner in Plate #12; both are C-series Steiners, although the one appearing here, at 22 inches, is a larger doll. But it is in the eyes that a more subtle difference surfaces. Plate #12 has classic blue threaded-glass "paperweight" eyes, while the larger Steiner's eyes are brown. Looking even more closely, one notices that the whites of her eyes are quite opaque and on the same plane as the irises. (The glass is rather deep over the irises of paperweight eyes, making a bulge that precludes movement in the socket.)

This mademoiselle is lucky to have what are called "wire eyes," a patented design by Steiner that enables the eyes to open and close by means of a wire protruding from the bisque head behind one ear, where it was unobtrusive beneath the doll's blond curls.

#51

The Kewpie doll is one of the most recognizable doll designs of the twentieth century until Barbie came along, that is. Designed by Rose O'Neill and patented in late 1912, the chubby little cherub was a nearly instantaneous hit. Anyone over the age of fifty can bring to mind the Kewpie's famous face: painted, curly-lashed wide eyes looking askance above a bump of a nose and a delightfully shy grin painted in a simple arc. Just a year after production started, twenty-one factories were churning out millions of little imps under license from Mrs. O'Neill and the Borgfeldt company in Germany.

This 18-inch tall German "googly" doll clearly comes from the Kewpie era. Her eyes both glance from side to side *and* open and close, in yet another development of eye design. Her five-piece composition body has the chunky proportions of a toddler, completing her appeal as an adorable character always ready for some harmless bit of mischief.

#53

Pensive, contemplative, wistful, dreamy, patient, serious, sad—the beholder can choose almost any mood to describe Kammer & Reinhardt's "Gretchen" and find it reflected in her small face. She has the soft lips and lovably pudgy cheeks of a toddler. Notice, however, that her expression emanates quietly from painted blue-grey eyes: no flashy patented moving parts here. But the resulting design is quite compelling even now, eighty-four years later. Most bisque doll styles were identified with numbers, and this one shows the number 114 incised on the back of her neck, one of an important series of character dolls made by Kammer & Reinhardt in the early 1900s. Gretchen is thought to have been modeled (and named) after a grandchild of Franz Reinhardt;[12] the same face, dressed as a boy, was marketed as Hans. Who, in 1910, could ever have dreamed that her value would soar to the $8,000 to $12,000 range by the 1990s?

People lucky enough to discover a doll or two in grandmother's trunk in the attic (an increasingly rare event!) are often surprised to learn that their little Oriental baby in embroidered silks or their Scots laddie complete with kilt actually started life in Germany, in spite of their detailed and authentic-looking costumes. Earlier in this century, as world-wide exploration continued to unveil exotic, even unknown cultures, national and native costumes closer to home were studied for their sociological interest. The middle class traveled as much as it could, and dolls in authentic local costumes became popular souvenirs.

These Dutch siblings were in fact made by C. M. Bergmann in Waltershausen, Germany, around 1915. C. M. Bergmann was himself well-traveled. Before launching his own doll-manufacturing business, he spent a number of years in the United States working as a miner and a cowboy.[13]

#54

#55

While American manufacturers, mostly in the Northeast, experimented with doll making in the second half of the nineteenth century, it was not until after World War I that Germany's dominance in the international doll market was eclipsed. In the teens and early twenties, the period this doll dates from, Germany's doll-making industry was enormously productive and cost-efficient, making their bisque dolls widely affordable to the middle class even after being shipped thousands of miles.

This staunch patriot, waving an early American flag, is thus a naturalized citizen, so to speak. She was made by the Gebrüder Krauss company in Eisfeld, a town in the heart of Germany's doll-making region. She is incised "Gbr 9 165 K." (Gebrüder is German for "brothers.") There were dozens of second-tier firms such as Krauss that produced perfectly lovely dolls, while never achieving the size of companies like Simon & Halbig or Kestner. Note that her blue sleeping eyes are ornamented with eyelashes. She stands 26 inches tall.

Simon & Halbig gets the credit for this genteel brunette admiring the fine quality of the embroidered white cotton lawn train of her wedding dress. The dress is actually a modern creation, but worked entirely from antique fabrics by her California owner. She has pierced ears, a common feature of turn-of-the-century bisque dolls, and a closed mouth designed to resemble French *bébés*. Notice the flexed wrists of her composition arms. In a 1910 report on German dolls, *McCall's Magazine* described the process of making composition body parts:

First the papier-mâché, in the form of a more or less dirty paste, is kneaded in a trough almost as bread is kneaded, until it reaches the proper consistency. Then . . . it is put into different machines and dolls' hands and sometimes also arms and legs are stamped out of it. It would certainly come near to breaking the heart of any especially tender-hearted little girl to stand in front of one of these machines while it was running at full speed and have her see a continuous stream of tiny hands pouring out of it . . . they look so pitiful and help-less, these miniature hands, almost as if they had been cut off of something alive.[14]

#56

#57

Simon & Halbig is also responsible for this slightly later bisque character baby, the sought-after mold number 1488, with its sleeping eyes, open/closed mouth, and five-piece bent-limb style body. This example, in her crisp, red-checked romper, retains her original wig.

The California collector who owns this doll has been collecting for about twenty-five years. She bought the doll illustrated here out of a local collection, and she has been "trading up" for years. One of the most unusual ways she obtained a doll came after she had given a talk to a nearby women's group on collecting antique dolls. The next day, her doorbell rang. A woman who had heard her speak the previous day was standing there, a bisque character baby in her arms, of which she insisted on giving to the collector! While doll lovers do enjoy exchanging information and collecting lore, it is certainly rare to be so well-rewarded.

This happily expectant face is "Hilda" by the German doll maker J. D. Kestner. Technically, she has sleeping eyes, an open mouth, and two upper teeth. Generally, she is simply entrancing, her face looking like it will break into a full smile at any moment.

Beginning in 1914, Hilda was made in several different versions. Molds 237 and 245 were sold with wigs, but an infant style was also offered with molded and painted hair. "Hilda" is usually, although not always, incised on the back of the neck, along with the mold number and "Ges. Gesch.," which is not a maker's name or mold designation, but an abbreviation of *"gesetzlich geschützt,"* a phrase meaning "registered." Many Hildas were sold with bent-limb composition bodies usually associated with babies, but this fresh-as-a-daisy example has a stocky ball-jointed toddler body. Hilda dolls with black and mulatto complexions have also been found, although rarely, and it is not known whether they were made around 1914 when production began, or sometime in the 1920s.

#58

#59

German character dolls became not only more lifelike and more realistically modeled, but sometimes more animated as well. The happy-go-lucky barefoot boy pictured here is another in Kammer & Reinhardt's famous character series, of which we have already met Gretchen (Plate #53). This jolly toddler measures a substantial 25 inches in height, and is marked *K ⬡ R* "Simon & Halbig 116/A." His dimples and grinning open/closed mouth make him a highly memorable face.

While all the Kammer & Reinhardt characters are quite valuable in today's market, that is not to say that they are *equally* valuable. Hildas (see page 104) can fetch prices in the $3,500 to $5,000 range at auction in the United States, mold 116s somewhat less, and Gretchens (Plate #53) sometimes a few thousand more. But the doll market hit an all-time high in London, in February, 1994 at Sotheby's, when a Kammer & Reinhardt character doll with painted eyes marked with mold number 108—the only example of this 1909 design currently known—sold at auction for an astonishing $279,000. A pouty-faced *K ⬡ R* 107 had prepared the way the year before in London, when a 21 inch example brought £33,000 at Christie's.

#60

Next in the series of Kammer & Reinhardt characters came *"Mein Liebling,"* or My Darling, marked "117." Available with open or closed mouths, they were produced from 1911 into the late 1920s. Here, she holds a small Stuart baby by Gebruder Heubach, whose flowered bonnet is molded in place. Note the baby's primitively molded arms in contrast to the well-finished composition hand of the K ✡ R doll.

German firms also experimented with faces that expressed more troubling emotions—a few infant designs appear to be downright screaming. This Kammer & Reinhardt, Simon & Halbig 115 is referred to by collectors as a pouty face and was made about the same time as *Mein Liebling*, but the diligent young seamstress, at 11 inches, is only half as tall.

#61

#62

Black bisque-head dolls are considerably scarcer than their white counterparts. This J. D. Kestner has a closed mouth, pierced ears (not an uncommon feature), and sleep eyes. She is believed to have been purchased in Paris in 1897, her current California owner says, and she may have been made in commemoration of Martinique's independence from France.

Nowadays, collectors distinguish between standard dolly faces given black complexions, as is the case here, and the rarer dolls with faces especially modeled with black facial features. For decades, those interested in black dolls could visit Aunt Len's Doll and Toy Museum in the Sugar Hill area of Harlem, New York, where the welcoming Lenon Holderhoyte showed generations of visitors the considerable variety of dolls in her collection. Aunt Len was committed to making her dolls available to the public. After her death, her estate negotiated with Sotheby's, New York, to put them up for sale at public auction in 1994.

Ever the pixie, this German bisque-head googly by Heubach features the side-glancing glass eyes that give the googly genre so much of its appeal. Although she looks the very picture of diminutive impishness, this doll stands 18 inches tall. How to display one's dolls—especially when the collecting bug has bitten hard, and there may be several hundred, or even thousands, to care for—continues to be a major concern for most collectors. Some solve the problem, at least to a degree, by trading their larger dolls for smaller examples in better condition or original dress. Most collectors opt to house their treasures inside glass cases, but those in earthquake-prone areas know that it is also a good idea to anchor those cases to the wall. Collectors in the Northeast have something else to worry about—humidity trapped inside the cases can cause precious costumes to mildew.

This chubby-cheeked toddler, 11 inches tall, has been wearing the same blue corduroy jacket and short pants since he was made circa 1910 by the prodigiously successful German firm of Armand Marseille. The company is known mostly for its enormous output—both of its own dolls, and heads and parts under contract to other concerns. Marseille's path to success was its quick, thrifty production, rather than painstaking quality control.

Nevertheless, Armand Marseille made some wonderful dolls, as this sprightly toddler can attest. When a doll is relatively more common, or comes from a manufacturer with a marginal reputation, condition becomes key. A common doll in pristine, original condition—even in the original box—has a special aura that surpasses its beginnings, and so can command a financial premium of triple, or perhaps quintuple, the value of a lesser example that shows wear. When a doll's head is cracked, its value is usually lessened by at least two thirds.

#65

Even when dolls are marked identically and come from the same mold, or series of molds, subtle differences make each doll distinct, as you can see by these twin Kestner googlies. Although it was undoubtedly a practiced hand applying important facial details, like the twins' high, slanting eyebrows which do so much for their expression of happy surprise, inflections of shading, or exact placement, are inevitable. Blushing on the cheeks of the same model of doll can vary considerably in tone, as can minor details, including dots for the nostrils, or the spacing of painted eyelashes.

Molds can show wear, as well. Crispness of modeling is important, especially for the later character dolls. The two *Mein Lieblings* at right are marked nearly identically—the larger is incised "117A," the smaller "117"—yet the modeling in the latter appears more sharply defined, and her bisque has a slightly higher sheen.

In this way, knowledgeable collectors must not only master cryptic numbers, symbols, and initials of maker's marks, but must also develop a good visual memory to be able to recognize surpassing quality.

#66

#67

Although the doll world reserves the word "character" to refer to rather realistically designed dolls from the teens and twenties, the twentieth century has spawned quite a number of dolls created in the likeness of *living* characters, which are called portrait dolls. The bisque-head Princess Elizabeth doll, for example, was made during the late twenties, to resemble the toddler who later became the Queen of England. Various admirals, including Dewey, inspired dolls for boys during the heyday of naval power. Additional characters, albeit imaginary ones, emerged from the increasingly popular comic strips, even as early as Palmer Cox's Brownie, starting in 1892.

The character represented here with his heart broken by a beautiful young German bisque-head dolly is Emmett Kelly, the world-famous clown known as "Willie the Tramp," a star of the Ringling Bros. and Barnum & Bailey Circus. He dates from the 1950s, and his extraordinarily modeled grimace is easily captured in vinyl.

Each era expresses itself in its toys and dolls, its customs and costumes, its rites of passage. In the 1860s, the *poupées* were ladylike adults, with corsets, hooped petticoats and serene expressions betraying nothing of the hustle and bustle of daily life. By the end of the century, the faces were those of idealized children, and by the 1960s, our culture was giving little girls a doll whose primary attributes were sexual: that classic American icon, Barbie.

It is not particularly surprising that collectors today so enjoy the character dolls of that middle period of the 1910s and 1920s, when the baby dolls looked like real babies and the toddlers like real toddlers. The birthday girl making her wish here is a 16-inch character named "Fany" by Armand Marseille. Helping her celebrate is a face the reader has already probably recognized: *Mein Liebling* by Kammer & Reinhardt.

#69

Because of the First and Second World Wars, Germany gradually lost its dominance in doll manufacture, while the culture of the United States set new trends from the movies to doll making. Less expensive and less fragile materials became important, and so various forms of composition were adapted from the twenties through the forties for dolls' heads as well as bodies.

The Alexander Doll Company, launched in 1926, became one of the most prominent American doll firms. Started by two sisters whose family had long been involved in doll making, they initially specialized in doll clothes. The "Madame Alexander" line of dolls, as they came to be known, included both literary characters and famous personalities, among them Scarlett O'Hara, the Little Women, the Dionne Quintuplets, and Snow White. With their permed curls, shadowed eyelids, and lipstick-kissed mouths, the faces of this 1940s bride and her maid of honor reveal the influence of American movies.

Doll collecting has mushroomed in the past thirty years. The United Federation of Doll Clubs, a non-profit group incorporated in 1949, believes that doll collecting may be the second largest hobby in the country. Interest has shifted over the years, from early nineteenth century dolls, to the classic French *bébés*, to German characters, all the way to American composition and vinyl dolls. Skyrocketing prices and ever-limited availability have influenced these slow shifts in taste and value.

During the sixties and seventies, a new category of doll arose: the contemporary, original creation of new designs in the classic material, bisque. These "doll artist dolls" have become a thriving market unto themselves, with an emphasis on limited editions and creative artistry. This handsome family of doll artist dolls bears witness to the possibilities of updating a wonderful tradition.

#70

Sometimes a doll is so appealing and yet so very rare that it is impossible for the doll to become available to the thousands of collectors who desire it. Two types of dolls solve this problem: the outright fake and the honestly labeled reproduction. Because a new mold can easily be made from an antique bisque head, both fakes intended to deceive and reproductions made to sell for reasonable prices are a permanent part of the doll market. The Albert Marque dolls pictured here do not date from 1915, but are reproductions.

All doll collecting pays homage to the past, both on a broad, cultural level and within the individual memories of collectors. Whether the driving impulse is historical interest or the pleasure of fulfilling a barely remembered longing, the net result is the same: the safeguarding of our collective past, face by face, treasure by treasure, doll by doll.

1. Dorothy S. Coleman et al., *The Collector's Encyclopedia of Dolls*, Vol. 2, (New York: Crown Publishers, 1986), 210.

2. Lynn Murray, "Les Bébés de la Maison Jumeau," *Antique Doll World*, Vol. 1, no. 1 (July/August 1993), 38.

3. Coleman, Vol. 1, *Encyclopedia of Dolls*, 96.

4. Lydia Richter, *Treasury of German Dolls* (HP Books, 1984), 32.

5. Coleman, Vol. 1, *Encyclopedia of Dolls*, 331.

6. Jurgen Cieslik and Marianne Cieslik, *German Doll Encyclopedia 1800–1939* (Hobby House Press, 1985), 153.

7. Murray, "Maison Jumeau," 38.

8. Coleman, Vol. 2, *Encyclopedia of Dolls*, 325.

9. Cieslik, *Doll Encyclopedia*, 199.

10. Ibid., 282.

11. Albert Alden, *A Present for Good Children* (Barre, Maine: Barre Publishers, 1834; reprint, Library of Congress, 1964).

12. Coleman, Vol. 2, *Encyclopedia of Dolls*, 612.

13. Cieslik, *Doll Encyclopedia*, 25.

14. Coleman, Vol. 2, *Encyclopedia of Dolls*, 776–777.